MODULAR **MIX**™

Edie Eckman

Annie's™

Module 2,
page 12

Module 5,
page 15

Module 3,
page 13

Table of Contents

Module 10,
page 20

Module 11,
page 21

Module 6,
page 16

Mixed Miters

Mitered squares make compelling knitting. They can be done quickly and often without a lot of thought, yet there are terrific design possibilities. Even novice knitters can get into the act, using nothing more complicated than knit stitches and k3tog decreases.

The basic idea is simple: The cast-on edge creates two sides of a square, then double decreases at the center of the knitting bends the cast-on edge, creating an approximately 90-degree corner. The result is that the selvage edges become the other two sides of the square, but the more exciting result is that simple stripes and other stitch patterns also turn into right-angle designs. Mix in simple stitch patterns and you have even more design options.

Furthermore, putting the mitered pieces together is a breeze! For the most part, you can simply pick up stitches from existing shapes and continue knitting.

This booklet provides 12 basic mitered designs, each in three sizes, as well as various decrease options, suggestions for color choices, and tips for making each mitered creation your own. Finally, the Modular Mix Afghan pattern brings together many of these techniques in one large project.

Materials
You can use any type of yarn for mitered knitting, although the weight of the yarn and your needle size will of course affect your gauge and the drape of the fabric you make.

In most cases straight needles or circular needles used for knitting back and forth will work, although for Module 8 you'll need a set of five double-point needles.

As you start to make the modules, a locking/opening stitch marker or two will be useful, although after you become familiar with the techniques you may find you don't need them as often.

Gauge & Module Size
With mitered knitting, gauge is often stated by giving the size of an entire module, rather than by stitches and rows. All sample modules were made using worsted-weight yarn and a size 9 (5.5mm)

needle. Three sizes of blocks are given. Numbers for the small block are given first, with numbers for the medium and large blocks in parentheses.

The beginning numbers for each module vary depending on the stitch pattern used in that module. While it would be easiest if the beginning numbers were the same for each size module, you would find that the characteristics of the stitches in that example might make the module smaller or larger than others with the same number of stitches. This isn't a problem with using the same module for an entire project, but it can be challenging when mixing stitch patterns modularly. Therefore, in this booklet each of the 12 modules has been designed to result in a piece that is roughly the same size so that they can be mixed and matched.

As a rule, modules that are predominantly garter stitch or seed stitch begin with 13 (26, 52) stitches per side, plus one (or more) corner stitch(es). Modules that are predominantly stockinette stitch, slip stitch or ribbing need a few more stitches and thus begin with 14 (28, 56) stitches per side, plus one (or more) corner stitch(es).

The three sizes presented in the book are based on using a worsted-weight yarn (CYCA 4-Medium) and size 9 (5.5mm) knitting needles. Sizes are approximate.

The finished sizes are:

Small square = 3 x 3 inches

Medium square = 6 x 6 inches

Large square = 12 x 12 inches

Your gauge and module size may be different based on your yarn and the number of stitches you choose to begin with.

Changing the Number of Stitches

The instructions for each module below tell you how many stitches to begin with, as well as the number of stitches for each side, but it's easy to change the number of stitches you begin with if you understand a little about the construction of the squares.

With the exception of Modules 7 and 8, the cast-on or beginning number is made up of one corner stitch, plus two sides with an equal number of stitches. To figure the number of stitches per side, just do a little math. Take the beginning number, subtract one corner stitch, then divide the resulting number by two to get the number of stitches per side.

105 cast-on stitches – 1 corner stitch = 104 stitches

104 stitches ÷ 2 sides = 52 stitches per side

Module 7 has two short sides and one long side that is twice as long as each short side, so 106 cast-on stitches – 2 corner stitches = 104 stitches

104 stitches ÷ 4 sides = 52 stitches per short side

52 stitches x 2 = 104 stitches per long side

Module 8 has four sides and four corners, so 212 cast-on stitches – 4 corner stitches = 208 stitches

208 stitches ÷ 4 sides = 52 stitches per side

Because of stitch patterning, some modules require that this starting number be a certain multiple of stitches on each side. For example, Module 6 requires beginning with a multiple of 4 plus 1 stitches. This could be 9, 13, 17 stitches, or any multiple of 4, plus 1: 4 x 20 = 80 stitches, plus 1 = 81 stitches.

Techniques

It's helpful to be familiar with several different types of cast-ons and double decreases in order to be able to choose the best one for a particular circumstance.

Long-tail cast-on: The long-tail cast-on creates a stable edge for beginning the first square. The first row after the cast-on will be a wrong-side row (see page 25 for directions).

Cable cast-on: The cable cast-on is a good choice for adding stitches to existing stitches already on the needle (see page 25 for directions).

Purl cable cast-on: In constructing mitered pieces that are connected, often you will need to cast on stitches so that the wrong side (purl side) of the cast-on is facing. This is where the purl cable cast-on comes in.

*With RS facing, insert the RH needle from back to front between the first 2 sts on LH needle, yo and draw a new st through between the existing sts; place new st onto LH needle; rep from * for desired number of cast-on sts.

Decreases

Each type of decrease described below creates a slightly different look. Experiment with all of them to see which you prefer. You may like the look of an all-garter stitch decrease, created by keeping the centered mitered stitch as a knit stitch on both right- and wrong-side rows, or you may prefer to purl the mitered stitch on wrong-side rows to create a more prominent stockinette stitch "spine" along the miter.

Using a stitch marker in the center stitch of the miter and moving it up on each row will help you keep track of where to put the decreases.

Knit 3 together (k3tog): Knit next 3 sts tog, yo and draw the new st through all 3 sts; drop 3 sts from LH needle.

When worked on the right side, this double decrease creates a right-leaning decrease on the right side.

P3tog (purl 3 together): Insert needle pwise into next 3 sts tog, yo and draw the new st through all 3 sts; drop 3 sts from LH needle.

When worked on the wrong side, this double decrease creates a right-leaning decrease on the right side.

PDD (purl double decrease): Slip next 2 sts one at a time kwise, insert LH needle from right to left into these same 2 sts and slip them back to LH needle tog, p3tog.

This double decrease is usually worked on the wrong side. It is a centered decrease, leaning to neither the left nor the right; viewed from the right side, the center stitch remains in the front center of the two decreased stitches.

S2pp (slip 2, purl 1, pass slipped sts over): Insert RH needle from left to right into back loops of next 2 sts tog and slip them to LH needle, p1, pass 2 slipped sts over the purl st.

This is another centered double decrease worked on the wrong side. As in the PDD, when viewed from the right side, the center stitch remains in the front center of the two decreased stitches. Use either the s2pp or the PDD, whichever you find easiest to execute.

S2kp (slip 2, knit 1, pass slipped sts over): Slip next 2 sts tog kwise, k1, pass 2 slipped sts over the knit st.

This double decrease is worked on the right side and creates a centered double decrease on the right side.

If you purl the center stitch on the wrong-side rows, you'll get a stockinette stitch miter on the right side. Note that if you use the stockinette stitch miter, you may find that the "spine" gets a bit too long in comparison with the stitches around it. If so, just take an extra decrease somewhere along the way.

Working From Previous Modules

One of the great things about mitered modules is that they can be picked up and knitted from existing modules. No seams needed! The arrangement of shapes and the order in which you knit them will offer different situations that require either casting on stitches, picking up all stitches from existing pieces, or some combination of picking up and casting on stitches.

The first module of any project will, of course, require you to cast on the full number of stitches, but from that point on, you'll be picking up stitches from existing modules. To pick up stitches from existing blocks, with right side facing, pick up one side's worth of stitches from the upper edge of one block, pick up one stitch in the corner between existing blocks, then pick up the remaining side's worth of stitches from the edge of the next block.

In the examples in this book, sometimes you'll be matching stitch-for-stitch and row-for-row in your pick-ups, but sometimes you will have to adjust the pick-up rate to be able to pick up the right number of stitches, depending on which block you are working. Sometimes you'll be casting on a portion of the stitches, then picking up stitches from an existing module. Other times you may be picking up stitches from an existing module or modules, then casting on additional stitches.

Directionality

The most prominent feature of a mitered module is the direction of the diagonal line of decreases. With the exception of Modules 7 and 8, all of the modules have a single diagonal line that runs from the center of the cast-on or beginning stitches outward.

You can change the direction of this line by choosing to pick up and work stitches not just from the lower and left edges, but from other directions as well. Look at these examples. The red line indicates the stitches that were cast on or picked up, while the black arrow shows the direction of the miter.

The Modules

Instructions for the modules are included on the following pages, along with tips and construction notes unique to each one. The photographed samples are all size medium. ●

You can change the direction of this line by choosing to pick up and work stitches not just from the lower and left edges, but from other directions as well. Look at these examples. The red line indicates the stitches that were cast on or picked up, while the arrow shows the direction of the miter.

Modular Mix Afghan

This Afghan uses all the module shapes and sizes together on one colorful project. If you find you don't like a particular color choice or module placement, choose another. There are plenty to choose from, or use your own colors to craft this one-of-a-kind afghan.

Skill Level
■■□□ EASY

Finished Measurement
48 x 60 inches

Materials
- Plymouth Yarn Encore (worsted weight; 75% acrylic/25% wool; 200 yds/100g ball): 4 balls each purple #452 (A), red #453 (B), pumpkin #175 (C), green #462 (D)
- Size 9 (5.5 mm) needles or size needed to obtain gauge
- Size 9 (5.5 mm) double-point needles (set of 5) for Module 8
- Locking stitch markers

Gauge
17 sts and 34 rows = 4 inches/10 cm in garter st.

17 sts and 26 rows = 4 inches in St st.

Small square = 3 inches; medium square = 6 inches; large square = 12 inches.

To save time, take time to check gauge.

Special Abbreviations
Knit 3 together (k3tog): Knit 3 sts tog.

Knit 5 together (k5tog): Knit 5 sts tog.

Purl double decrease (PDD): Slip next 2 sts one at a time kwise, insert LH needle from right to left into these same 2 sts and slip them back to LH needle, p3tog.

Purl 3 together (p3tog): Purl 3 sts tog.

Slip 1, knit 2 together, pass slipped stitch over (s2kp): Slip next 2 sts tog kwise, k1, pass 2 slipped sts over to dec 2 sts.

Special Technique
Purl Cable Cast-On: *Insert needle from back to front between first 2 sts on LH needle, yo and draw a new st through between the existing sts; place new st onto LH needle; rep from * for desired number of cast-on sts.

Pattern Notes
Afghan is worked in sections, picking up stitches from previous squares. Read general instructions for mitered blocks before beginning.

There are 20 large Blocks (A–T) in the afghan; some of these blocks are a single large module, while others are made up of a number of small and medium modules. Refer to the assembly diagram and block detail diagram for the order of knitting the pieces. The first several blocks are described in detail, while subsequent blocks are presented graphically. Refer to photo for color sequence, or create your own.

In the block detail diagram, the number in each block refers to the Module number (1–12) and the letter refers to the size (S, M, L). The red line indicates the beginning stitches of the module, while the black line indicates the direction of the miter.

Block A
Long-tail cast on 105 sts for large size.

Work Module 2 to end, changing colors as indicated in photo or making your own color choices.

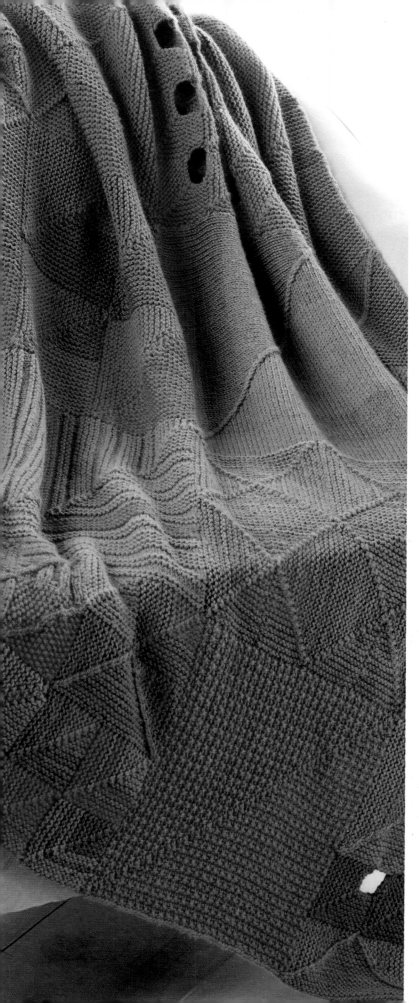

Block B

This block is made up of several small- and medium-sized modules. It is one of the more challenging ones to work because it includes many different modules, but it helps you to understand the way the rest of the afghan is structured. After this block, you'll find the others easy to work.

Refer to the block detail diagram (page 10); the small red numbers indicate the order in which the modules are worked, as described below:

1. Pm halfway up right edge of Block A. Long-tail cast on 26 sts, pick up and knit 1 st at lower right corner of Block A, pick up and knit 26 sts evenly spaced to marker, remove marker—53 sts for Module 3 medium size. Pm in center st and move it up each row. Work Module 3 to end.

2. Pm at right edge of Block A, halfway between previous module and top edge of Block A. With RS facing, beg at center top of previous module, pick up and knit 14 sts along top edge of previous module, pick up and knit 1 st in corner, pick up and knit 14 sts evenly spaced along Block A to marker, remove marker—29 sts for Module 4 small size. Work Module 4 to end.

3. With RS facing, beg at upper right corner of previous module, pick up and knit 13 sts along top edge of previous module, pick up and knit 1 st in corner, pick up and knit 13 sts evenly spaced along Block A to corner—27 sts for Module 1 small size. Work Module 1 to end.

4. Pick up and knit 14 sts along rem top edge of first module in this Block, pick up and knit 1 st in corner, pick up and knit 14 sts to corner—29 sts for Module 11 size small. Work Module 11 to end.

5. Pick up and knit 13 sts along top edge of previous module, pick up and knit 1 st in corner, pick up and knit 13 sts to corner—29 sts for Module 5 size small. Work Module 5 to end.

6. Pm halfway up right edge of medium module. Long-tail cast on 13 sts, pick up and knit 1 st in lower corner of module, pick up and knit 13 sts evenly spaced to marker, remove marker—27 sts for Module 1 size small. Work Module 1 to end.

7–9. Continue in this manner to work three additional small modules.

10. Long-tail cast on 13 sts, pick up and knit 1 st in corner of last module, pick up and knit 26 sts along top edge of 2 small modules, pick up and knit 1 st in corner, pick up and knit 13 sts in next module to corner—54 sts for Module 7 size small. Work Module 7 to end.

11. Beg at center top of previous module, pick up and knit 13 sts along top edge of previous module, pick up and knit 1 st in corner, pick up and knit 13 sts evenly spaced along Block A to corner—27 sts for Module 1 small size. Work Module 1 to end.

12. Beg at corner of Module 7, pick up and knit 13 sts along top edge of module, pick up and knit 1 st in corner, pick up and knit 13 sts along previous module to corner—27 sts for Module 1 small size. Work Module 1 to end.

Block C
Long-tail cast on 56 sts, pick up and knit 1 st in corner of Block B, pick up and knit 56 sts evenly spaced along edge of Block B—113 sts for Module 6 large size. Work Module 6 to end.

Block D
1. Pms ¼ and ½ the way up right edge of Block C. Long-tail cast on 40 sts, pick up and knit 1 st at lower right corner of Block C, pick up and knit 13 sts evenly spaced to first marker, remove first marker—54 sts for Module 7 small size. Work Module 7 to end.

2. Beg at center top of previous module, pick up and knit 13 sts along top edge of previous module, pick up and knit 1 st in corner, pick up and knit 13 sts evenly spaced along Block C to marker, remove marker—27 sts for Module 9 small size. Work Module 9 to end.

3. Beg at upper right corner of first module, pick up and knit 13 sts along top edge of rectangle, pick up and knit 1 st in corner, pick up and knit 7 sts evenly spaced along previous module to corner, turn; Purl Cable Cast On 6 sts—27 sts for Module 9 small size. Work Module 9 to end.

4. Long-tail cast on 26 sts, pick up and knit 1 st in corner, pick up and knit 20 sts along side edges of rectangle and small square; turn; Purl Cable Cast On 6 sts—53 sts for Module 11 medium size. Work Module 11 to end.

5. Long-tail cast on 26 sts, pick up and knit 1 st in upper right corner of previous module, pick up and knit 26 sts evenly spaced across top of medium-module; turn; Purl Cable Cast On 6 sts, turn; pick up and knit 7 sts evenly spaced along top of first small module; turn; Purl Cable Cast On 6 sts, turn; pick up and knit 7 sts evenly spaced along top of second

small module; pick up and knit 1 st in corner, pick up and knit 26 sts along remaining side of Block C—106 sts for Module 7 medium size.

Blocks E & F
Refer to block detail diagram (page 10) and module explanations to add Blocks E and F.

Block G
Pms at top center of Block C and at center of right edge of Block F. Beg at a point halfway between marked st on Block C and corner, and using dpns, pick up and knit 13 sts to corner, pick up and knit 1 st in corner, pick up and knit 26 sts evenly spaced to marker; turn, Purl Cable Cast On 54 sts, pick up and knit 1 st at center top edge of Block C, pick up and knit 13 sts to beginning—108 sts for Module 8 size medium. Work Module 8 to end.

Work rem modules in this block in the same manner.

Blocks H–T
Continue, referring to block detail diagram and module explanations to add Blocks H through T.

Finishing
Weave in ends. Steam block lightly. •

Block Q	Block R	Block S	Block T
Block M	Block N	Block O	Block P
Block I	Block J	Block K	Block L
Block E	Block F	Block G	Block H
Block A	Block B	Block C	Block D

AFGHAN ASSEMBLY DIAGRAM
Work blocks in order shown, starting with Block A and ending with Block T.

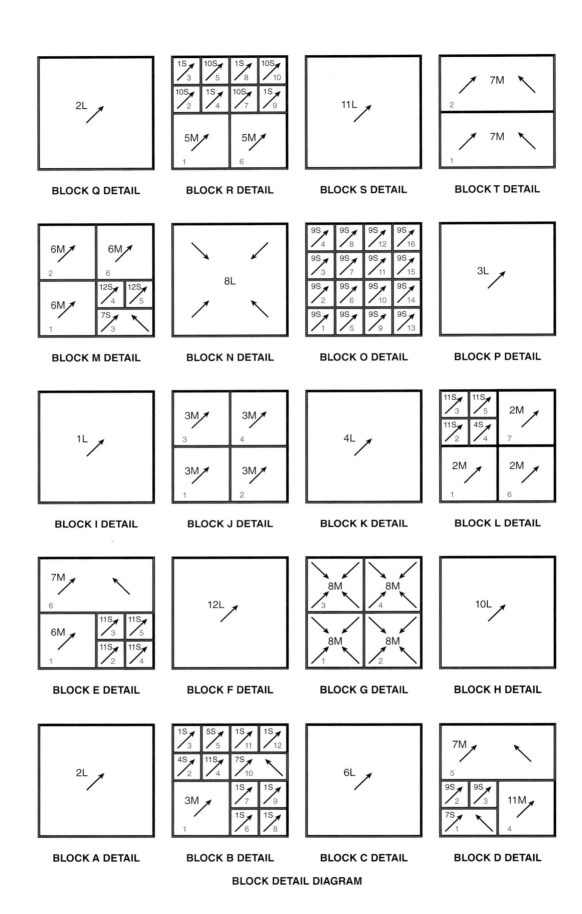

BLOCK Q DETAIL

BLOCK R DETAIL

BLOCK S DETAIL

BLOCK T DETAIL

BLOCK M DETAIL

BLOCK N DETAIL

BLOCK O DETAIL

BLOCK P DETAIL

BLOCK I DETAIL

BLOCK J DETAIL

BLOCK K DETAIL

BLOCK L DETAIL

BLOCK E DETAIL

BLOCK F DETAIL

BLOCK G DETAIL

BLOCK H DETAIL

BLOCK A DETAIL

BLOCK B DETAIL

BLOCK C DETAIL

BLOCK D DETAIL

BLOCK DETAIL DIAGRAM

Module 1: Garter Square (multiple of 2 + 1)

This is the easiest and most basic square—perfect for beginners. Try it with stripes or larger blocks of color for variety. To make it larger or smaller, you can use any number of stitches per side on this versatile square.

. . . .

Color Sequence

The featured module uses the following colors:

Cast-on and Rows 1–3 (A)

Rows 4–9 (B)

Rows 10–17 (C)

Rows 18–27 (D)

Rows 28–52 (A)

Module 1

Cast on 27 (53, 105) sts [13 (26, 52) sts per side + 1 corner st]. Pm in center st and move it up each row.

Row 1 (WS): Knit.

Row 2: Knit to 1 st before marked st, k3tog, knit to end—2 sts dec.

Rep Rows 1 and 2 until 3 sts rem, ending with a WS row.

Last row: K3tog—1 st.

Fasten off. ●

Module 2: Garter Square With Stockinette Stitch (multiple of 2 + 1)

Here the basic garter stitch square is worked using a centered stockinette stitch decrease that creates a more dramatic miter. Don't forget to work a purl stitch in the center stitch on the wrong side to keep it in pattern.

Pattern Note

Note: The stockinette stitch decrease creates a slightly longer diagonal line than the garter-stitch based decreases; you may find you want to decrease on wrong-side rows once or twice on the large square to shorten the mitered line a bit.

Color Sequence

The featured module uses the following colors:

Cast-on and Rows 1–3 (D)

Rows 4 and 5 (B)

Rows 6 and 7 (A)

Rows 8 and 9 (C)

Rows 10 and 11 (D)

Rows 12 and 13 (B)

Rows 14 and 15 (A)

Rows 16 and 17 (C)

Rows 18 and 19 (D)

Rows 20 and 21 (B)

Rows 22 and 23 (A)

Rows 24 and 25 (C)

Rows 26–52 (D)

Module 2

Cast on 27 (53, 105) sts [13 (26, 52) sts per side + 1 corner st]. Pm in center st and move it up each row.

Row 1 (WS): Knit to marked st, p1, knit to end.

Row 2: Knit to 1 st before marked st, s2kp, knit to end—2 sts dec.

Rep Rows 1 and 2 until 3 sts rem, ending with a WS row.

Last row: S2kp—1 st.

Fasten off. ●

Module 3: Garter Square With Yarn Overs (multiple of 2 + 1)

Simple yarn overs flank the multiple decreases in this variation on the basic garter square.

. . . .

Color Sequence
The featured module uses the following colors:

Cast-on and Rows 1–3 (C)

Rows 4 and 5 (B)

Rows 6 and 7 (A)

Rows 8 and 9 (D)

Rows 10 and 11 (B)

Rows 12 and 13 (A)

Rows 14 and 15 (D)

Rows 16–19 (C)

Rows 20 and 21 (B)

Rows 22 and 23 (D)

Rows 24 and 25 (A)

Rows 26 and 27 (B)

Rows 28 and 29 (D)

Rows 30 and 31 (A)

Rows 32–35 (C)

Rows 36 and 37 (D)

Rows 38 and 39 (A)

Rows 40 and 41 (B)

Rows 42–49 (C)

Module 3
Cast on 27 (53, 105) sts [13 (26, 52) sts per side + 1 corner st]. Pm in center st and move it up each row.

Row 1 (WS): Knit.

Row 2: Knit to 2 sts before marked st, yo, k5tog, yo, knit to end—2 sts dec.

Rep Rows 1 and 2 until 5 sts rem, ending with a WS row.

Last row: K5tog—1 st.

Fasten off. ●

Module 4: Stockinette Square (multiple of 2 + 1)

Unlike garter stitch, which has one stitch for every two rows (i.e. one ridge), stockinette stitch has rectangular stitches: The width of the stitch is greater than the height of the stitch. This relationship of stitches to rows means that, in order to have a nicely squared miter, decreases have to take place every two out of three rows. While these right-side and wrong-side decreases can be any combination of the options listed above, the sample shown here uses a centered stockinette stitch double decrease on both the right side and wrong side.

Another feature of stockinette stitch is its tendency to roll at the edges. Blocking your piece will help, but when used in a project, the edge will require either the addition of a non-rolling border, or placement of the stockinette stitch square surrounded by other, non-rolling pieces.

· ·

Color Sequence
The featured module uses the following colors:

Cast-on and Rows 1–3 (B)

Rows 4–7 (D)

Rows 8–11 (A)

Rows 12–15 (B)

Rows 16–19 (D)

Rows 20–23 (A)

Rows 24–27 (B)

Rows 28–31 (A)

Rows 32–35 (D)

Rows 36–39 (B)

Module 4
Cast on 29 (57, 113) sts [14 (28, 56) sts per side + 1 corner st]. Pm in center st and move it up each row.

Row 1 (WS): Purl.

Row 2: Knit to 1 st before marked st, s2kp, knit to end—2 sts dec.

Row 3: Purl to 1 st before marked st, PDD, purl to end—2 sts dec.

Row 4: Knit.

Row 5: Purl to 1 st before marked st, PDD, purl to end—2 sts dec.

Row 6: Knit to 1 st before marked st, s2kp, knit to end—2 sts dec.

Continue in this manner to dec 2 sts every 2 rows out of 3, until 1 st rem.

Fasten off. ●

Module 5: 2x2 Ribbed Square (multiple of 4 + 1)

You probably already know that ribbing pulls in, and this module is no exception. In its original, unblocked state, it looks like an entirely different shape. Try using it in this format, connected to other ribbed modules, and see what your fabric looks like. You may be surprised and thrilled!

To use it as a "square," however, block the module carefully, and place it among other shapes—different modules or a shape-holding edging—to force the ribs to open up and show off.

Color Sequence
The featured module uses C throughout.

Module 5
Cast on 29 (57, 113) sts [13 (26, 52) sts each side + 1 corner st]. Pm in center st and move it up each row.

Row 1 (WS): (P2, k2) to 2 (0, 0) sts before marked st, p5 (1, 1), (k2, p2) to end.

Row 2: (K2, p2) to 2 (4, 4) sts before marked st, k1 (2, 2), p0 (1, 1), s2kp, p0 (1, 1), k1 (2, 2), (p2, k2) to end—2 sts dec.

Row 3: (P2, k2) to 1 (3, 3) sts before marked st, p0 (2, 2), PDD, p0 (2, 2), (k2, p2) to end—2 sts dec.

Row 4: (K2, p2) to 0 (2, 2) sts before marked st, k1 (5, 5), (p2, k2) to end.

Row 5: (P2, k2) to 4 (2, 2) sts before marked st, p2 (1, 1), k1 (0, 0), PDD, k1 (0, 0), p2 (1, 1), (k2, p2) to end—2 sts dec.

Row 6: (K2, p2) to 3 (1, 1) sts before marked st, k2 (0, 0), s2kp, k2 (0, 0), (p2, k2) to end—2 sts dec.

Row 7: (P2, k2) to 2 (0, 0) sts before marked st, p 5 (1, 1), (k2, p2) to end.

Rep Rows 2–7 until 3 sts rem, ending with a WS row.

Last row: S2kp—1 st.

Fasten off. ●

Module 6: Slip Stitch Square (multiple of 4 + 1)

Slip stitch is a great way to mix colors while still just using one color per row. However, it does create a fabric with more stitches and rows per inch than its garter stitch or stockinette stitch cousins. Therefore, this slip-stitch module uses a few more beginning stitches to create the same size square.

· ·

Color Sequence
The featured module uses the following colors:

Cast-on and Row 1 (B)

Rows 2 and 3 (D)

Rows 4 and 5 (B)

Continue working 2 rows of alternating colors, making the last row in B.

Module 6
Note: Slip all sts pwise with yarn on WS.

With MC, cast on 29 (57, 113) sts [14 (28, 56) sts per side + 1 corner st]. Pm in center st and move it up each row.

Row 1 (WS): Knit.

Row 2: With CC, (k1, sl 1) to 2 sts before marked st, k1, k3tog, k1, (sl 1, k1) to end—2 sts dec.

Row 3: (K1, sl 1) to 1 st before marked st, k3, (sl 1, k1) to end.

Row 4: With MC, knit to 1 st before marked st, k3tog, knit to end—2 sts dec.

Rep Rows 1–4 until 3 sts rem, ending with a WS row.

Last row: With MC, k3tog.

Fasten off. ●

Module 7: Rectangle With Stockinette Stitch Center (multiple of 4 + 2)

This rectangle is the size of two squares, with the miters running toward each other. Only two sizes are given here, small (medium), as the "large" size would be truly large—the size of two large squares! This sample uses a stockinette stitch miter, but use whatever decrease you prefer.

. . . .

Color Sequence
The featured module uses the following colors:

Cast-on and Rows 1–9 (D)

Rows 10 and 11 (A)

Rows 12–15 (D)

Rows 16 and 17 (C)

Rows 18–21 (A)

Rows 22 and 23 (B)

Rows 24–27 (A)

Rows 28 and 29 (C)

Rows 30–33 (D)

Rows 34 and 35 (A)

Rows 36–51 (D)

Module 7
Cast on 54 (106) sts [13 (26) sts per short side + 26 (52) sts per long side + 2 corner sts]. Pm in 14th (27th) st from each end and move them up each row.

Row 1 (WS): (Knit to marked st, p1) twice, knit to end.

Row 2: (Knit to 1 st before marked st, s2kp) twice, knit to end—4 sts dec.

Rep Rows 1 and 2 until 6 sts rem, ending with a WS row.

Last row: (S2kp) twice—2 sts. Cut yarn and thread end through rem sts.

Pull tight and fasten off. ●

Module 8: 4-Mitered Square (multiple of 4)

Work this square in the round using double-point needles. You may find it easier to begin the larger square on circular needles, then change to double-point needles as the circumference decreases.

The beginning of the round is in the middle of one side of the square, with the marked stitches in the center of each double-point needle. This takes some planning when picking up stitches from previously knit modules; you'll probably need to pick up half of the side stitches, then a corner stitch, then all the stitches along the next side, then cast on for two more sides, then pick up the remaining half of the first-side stitches. See the Modular Mix Afghan for an example.

. . . .

Color Sequence
The featured module uses the following colors:

Cast-on and Rnds 1–3 (A)

Rnds 4–7 (B)

Rnds 8–11 (A)

Rnds 12–15 (B)

Rnds 16–19 (A)

Rnds 20–23 (B)

Rnds 24–27 (A)

Module 8
Cast on 56 (108, 212) sts [13 (26, 52) sts per side + 4 corner sts]. Counting from 1 edge, place four markers as follows and move them up each rnd:

Small: 7th, 21st, 35th and 49th sts

Medium: 14th, 41st, 68th and 95th sts

Large: 27th, 80th, 133rd and 186th sts

Divide sts evenly onto 4 needles, with the marked st in the center of each needle. Beg working in the rnd.

Rnd 1: Purl.

Rnd 2: (Knit to 1 st before marked st, s2kp) 4 times, knit to end—8 sts dec.

Rep Rnds 1 and 2 until 8 (4, 4) sts rem, ending with a purl rnd.

Small Size Only
Last rnd: (K2tog) around—4 sts.

Cut yarn, leaving a 6-inch tail. Weave tail through rem sts and pull tight. ●

Module 9: Partial Garter Square (multiple of 2 + 1)

When you stop knitting a square before it's a square, you get this wonderful partial square. These instructions tell you to knit until about half the stitches are gone, but you'll want to play around with other options.

When picking up stitches from this module, you'll have to do some combination of picking up and casting on stitches, or vice versa. See the Modular Mix Afghan for an example.

. . . .

Color Sequence
The featured module uses the following colors:

Cast-on and Rows 1–28 (A)

Row 29 and bind-off (B)

Module 9
Cast on 27 (53, 105) sts [13 (26, 52) sts per side + 1 corner st]. Pm in center st and move it up each row.

Row 1 (WS): Knit.

Row 2: Knit to 1 st before marked st, k3tog, knit to end—2 sts dec.

Rep Rows 1 and 2 until 13 (27, 53) sts (or desired number) rem, ending with a RS row. Bind off kwise on WS. ●

Module 10: Garter Stitch & Eyelets Square (multiple of 4 + 1)

A little lace is always fun, and lace doesn't get simpler than a (yo, k2tog) combination. This is another module that looks better with a bit of blocking to open up the eyelets.

· ·

Color Sequence

The featured module uses D throughout.

Module 10

Cast on 29 (53, 105) sts [14 (26, 52) sts per side + 1 corner st]. Pm in center st and move it up each row.

Rows 1 and 3 (WS): Knit.

Row 2: Knit to 1 st before marked st, s2kp, knit to end—2 sts dec.

Row 4: K1, (yo, k2tog) to 2 sts before marked st, k1, s2kp, k1, (ssk, yo) to last st, k1—2 sts dec.

Row 5: Purl.

Row 6: Rep Row 2—2 sts dec.

Row 7: Knit.

Row 8: Rep Row 4—2 sts dec.

Row 9: Purl to 1 st before marked st, PDD, purl to end—2 sts dec.

Row 10: Rep Row 2—2 sts dec.

Row 11: Knit.

Row 12: K1, (yo, k2tog) to 1 st before marked st, s2kp, (ssk, yo) to last st, k1—2 sts dec.

Row 13: Purl.

Row 14: Rep Row 2—2 sts dec.

Row 15: Knit.

Row 16: Rep Row 12—2 sts dec.

Row 17: Rep Row 9—2 sts dec.

Rep [Rows 2–17] 0 (1, 3) time(s), then rep [Rows 2–3 (2–7, 2–15)] once more—7 (7, 9) sts.

Rep Rows 2 and 3 until 3 sts rem.

Last row: S2kp.

Fasten off. ●

Module 11: Seed Stitch Square (multiple of 4 + 1)

Seed stitch is one of the most beautiful textured stitches, and it works wonderfully well on a mitered shape. If you prefer, use a k3tog decrease or other non-stockinette stitch miter to avoid interrupting the seed stitch texture. If you find the square getting skewed due to a too-long miter, stop when five stitches remain, and decrease all five stitches at once as follows: slip next three stitches together knitwise, k2tog, pass 3 slipped stitches over.

Color Sequence
The featured module uses the following colors:

Cast-on and Rows 1–7 (B)

Rows 8 and 9 (A)

Rows 10–17 (C)

Rows 18 and 19 (A)

Rows 20–27 (D)

Rows 28 and 29 (A)

Rows 30–51 (B)

Module 11
Cast on 29 (53, 105) sts [14 (26, 52) sts per side + 1 corner st]. Pm in center st and move it up each row.

Row 1: P1, (k1, p1) to end.

Row 2: (P1, k1) to 2 sts before marked st, p1, s2kp, p1, (k1, p1) to end—2 sts dec.

Row 3: (P1, k1) to 1 st before marked st, p3, (k1, p1) to end.

Row 4: (P1, k1) to 1 st before marked st, s2kp, (k1, p1) to end—2 sts dec.

Rep Rows 1–4 until 3 sts rem, ending with a WS row.

Last row: S2kp.

Fasten off. ●

Module 12: Garter Welts Square (multiple of 2 + 1)

A garter stitch square with a few purl rows mixes textures. Although it's shown in a solid color here, try making the stockinette stitch portions in a different color for even more interest.

. . . .

Color Sequence
The featured module uses C throughout.

Module 12
Cast on 27 (53, 105) sts [13 (26, 52) sts per side + 1 corner st]. Pm in center st and move it up each row.

Row 1 (WS): Knit.

Row 2: Knit to 1 st before marked st, k3tog, knit to end—2 sts dec.

Rows 3 and 4: Rep Rows 1 and 2—2 sts dec.

Row 5: Purl.

Row 6: Rep Row 2—2 sts dec.

Rows 7–10: Rep [Rows 1 and 2] twice—4 sts dec.

Row 11: Purl to 1 st before marked st, p3tog, purl to end—2 sts dec.

Row 12: Rep Row 2.

Rows 13–16: Rep [Rows 1 and 2] twice—4 sts dec.

Rep [Rows 1–16] 0 (1, 4) time(s), then rep [Rows 1 and 2] until 3 sts rem, ending with a WS row.

Last row: K3tog.

Fasten off. •

General Information

Abbreviations & Symbols

[ ] work instructions within brackets as many times as directed

( ) work instructions within parentheses in the place directed

** repeat instructions following the asterisks as directed

* repeat instructions following the single asterisk as directed

" inch(es)

approx approximately
beg begin/begins/beginning
CC contrasting color
ch chain stitch
cm centimeter(s)
cn cable needle
dec(s) decrease/decreases/ decreasing
dpn(s) double-point needle(s)
g gram(s)
inc(s) increase/increases/ increasing

k knit
k2tog knit 2 stitches together
kfb knit in front and back
kwise knitwise
LH left hand
m meter(s)
M1 make one stitch
MC main color
mm millimeter(s)
oz ounce(s)
p purl
p2tog purl 2 stitches together
pat(s) pattern(s)
pm(s) place marker(s)
psso pass slipped stitch over
pwise purlwise
rem remain/remains/remaining
rep(s) repeat(s)
rev St st reverse stockinette stitch
RH right hand
rnd(s) rounds
RS right side

skp slip, knit, pass slipped stitch over—1 stitch decreased
sk2p slip 1, knit 2 together, pass slipped stitch over the knit 2 together—2 stitches decreased
sl slip
sl 1 kwise slip 1 knitwise
sl 1 pwise slip 1 purlwise
sl st slip stitch(es)
ssk slip, slip, knit these 2 stitches together—a decrease
st(s) stitch(es)
St st stockinette stitch
tbl through back loop(s)
tog together
WS wrong side
wyib with yarn in back
wyif with yarn in front
yd(s) yard(s)
yfwd yarn forward
yo (yo's) yarn over(s)

Standard Yarn Weight System
Categories of yarn, gauge ranges and recommended needle sizes.

Yarn Weight Symbol & Category Names	0 LACE	1 SUPER FINE	2 FINE	3 LIGHT	4 MEDIUM	5 BULKY	6 SUPER BULKY
Type of Yarns in Category	Fingering 10-Count Crochet Thread	Sock, Fingering, Baby	Sport, Baby	DK, Light Worsted	Worsted, Afghan, Aran	Chunky, Craft, Rug	Super Chunky, Roving
Knit Gauge Range* in Stockinette Stitch to 4 inches	33–40 sts**	27–32 sts	23–26 sts	21–24 sts	16–20 sts	12–15 sts	6–11 sts
Recommended Needle in Metric Size Range	1.5–2.25mm	2.25–3.25mm	3.25–3.75mm	3.75–4.5mm	4.5–5.5mm	5.5–8mm	8mm and larger
Recommended Needle U.S. Size Range	000 to 1	1 to 3	3 to 5	5 to 7	7 to 9	9 to 11	11 and larger

* **GUIDELINES ONLY:** The above reflect the most commonly used gauges and needle sizes for specific yarn categories.

** Lace weight yarns are usually knitted on larger needles and hooks to create lacy, openwork patterns. Accordingly, a gauge range is difficult to determine. Always follow the gauge stated in your pattern.

Inches Into Millimeters & Centimeters
All measurements are rounded off slightly.

inches	mm	cm	inches	cm	inches	cm	inches	cm
⅛	3	0.3	5	12.5	21	53.5	38	96.5
¼	6	0.6	5½	14	22	56.0	39	99.0
⅜	10	1.0	6	15.0	23	58.5	40	101.5
½	13	1.3	7	18.0	24	61.0	41	104.0
⅝	15	1.5	8	20.5	25	63.5	42	106.5
¾	20	2.0	9	23.0	26	66.0	43	109.0
⅞	22	2.2	10	25.5	27	68.5	44	112.0
1	25	2.5	11	28.0	28	71.0	45	114.5
1¼	32	3.2	12	30.5	29	73.5	46	117.0
1½	38	3.8	13	33.0	30	76.0	47	119.5
1¾	45	4.5	14	35.5	31	79.0	48	122.0
2	50	5.0	15	38.0	32	81.5	49	124.5
2½	65	6.5	16	40.5	33	84.0	50	127.0
3	75	7.5	17	43.0	34	86.5		
3½	90	9.0	18	46.0	35	89.0		
4	100	10.0	19	48.5	36	91.5		
4½	115	11.5	20	51.0	37	94.0		

Knitting Basics

Long-Tail Cast-On

Leaving an end about an inch long for each stitch to be cast on, make a slip knot on the right needle.

Place the thumb and index finger of your left hand between the yarn ends with the long yarn end over your thumb, and the strand from the skein over your index finger. Close your other fingers over the strands to hold them against your palm. Spread your thumb and index fingers apart and draw the yarn into a "V."

Place the needle in front of the strand around your thumb and bring it underneath this strand. Carry the needle over and under the strand on your index finger.

Draw through loop on thumb.

Drop the loop from your thumb and draw up the strand to form a stitch on the needle.

Repeat until you have cast on the number of stitches indicated in the pattern. Remember to count the beginning slip knot as a stitch.

Cable Cast-On

This type of cast-on is used when adding stitches in the middle or at the end of a row.

Make a slip knot on the left needle. Knit a stitch in this knot and place it on the left needle. Insert the right needle between the last two stitches on the left needle. Knit a stitch and place it on the left needle. Repeat for each stitch needed.

Knit (k)

Insert tip of right needle from front to back in next stitch on left needle.

Bring yarn under and over the tip of the right needle.

Pull yarn loop through the stitch with right needle point.

Slide the stitch off the left needle. The new stitch is on the right needle.

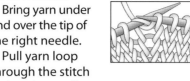

Purl (p)

With yarn in front, insert tip of right needle from back to front through next stitch on the left needle.

Bring yarn around the right needle counterclockwise. With right needle, draw yarn back through the stitch.

Slide the stitch off the left needle. The new stitch is on the right needle.

Bind-Off

Binding off (knit)
Knit first two stitches on left needle. Insert tip of left needle into first stitch worked on right needle and pull it over the second stitch and completely off the needle.

Knit the next stitch and repeat. When one stitch remains on right needle, cut yarn and draw tail through last stitch to fasten off.

Binding off (purl)
Purl first two stitches on left needle. Insert tip of left needle into first stitch worked on right needle and pull it over the second stitch and completely off the needle.

Purl the next stitch and repeat. When one stitch remains on right needle, cut yarn and draw tail through last stitch to fasten off.

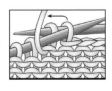

Decrease (dec)

Knit 2 together (k2tog)
Put tip of right needle through next two stitches on left needle as to knit. Knit these two stitches as one.

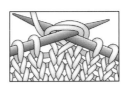

Purl 2 together (p2tog)
Put tip of right needle through next two stitches on left needle as to purl. Purl these two stitches as one.

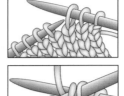

Slip, Slip, Knit (ssk)
Slip next two stitches, one at a time, as to knit from left needle to right needle.

Insert left needle in front of both stitches and knit them together.

Slip, Slip, Purl (ssp)
Slip next two stitches, one at a time, as to knit from left needle to right needle. Slip these stitches back onto left needle keeping them twisted. Purl these two stitches together through back loops.

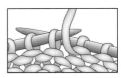

Meet the Designer

Edie is a designer, author and teacher who loves both knitting and crochet. She travels extensively to teach at conventions, shops and guilds around the country.

Her articles and designs have appeared in many yarn company publications, pattern books and magazines.

Edie is the author of a number of books including *Socks to Knit for Those You Love*, *Beyond the Square Crochet Motifs*, *I Can Knit* and *Connect the Shapes Crochet Motifs*.

Special Thanks

Special thanks to Plymouth Yarn Company for supplying the lovely yarn for this book. We had such a great time picking out colors! And many, many thanks to Super Knitter Barbara Kreuter, who knit the afghan under an impossibly short deadline and with minimal instruction from the designer.

Plymouth Yarn Co.
500 Lafayette St.
Bristol, PA 19007
(215) 788-0459
www.plymouthyarn.com

Photo Index

11

12

13

14

6

15

16

17

18

19

20

21

22

 ™ *Modular Mix* is published by Annie's, 306 East Parr Road, Berne, IN 46711. Printed in USA. Copyright © 2012 Annie's.
All rights reserved. This publication may not be reproduced in part or in whole without written permission from the publisher.

RETAIL STORES: If you would like to carry this pattern book or any other Annie's publications, visit AnniesWSL.com.

Every effort has been made to ensure that the instructions in this pattern book are complete and accurate. We cannot, however, take responsibility
for human error, typographical mistakes or variations in individual work. Please visit AnniesCustomerCare.com to check for pattern updates.

ISBN: 978-1-59635-682-5
1 2 3 4 5 6 7 8 9